CANINE IN THE PROMISED LAND

CANINE IN THE PROMISED LAND

POEMS

PHILIP J. KOWALSKI

atmosphere press

CONTENTS

THE TIP OF THE ICEBERG

We've been so fond of saying
"That's just the tip of the iceberg,"
As if we've said something clever,
When it's really a tired cliché.

And when the polar caps completely melt,
And the glaciers no longer hold sway,
And the tip of the iceberg is reduced to water,
What will we then have to say?

"That's just the [fill in the blank],"
As we struggle to articulate
The ravages of the earth
That we have shamelessly betrayed.

FIELD MOUSE

It was just
A little black
Field mouse
That arrived
From what was
Then virgin forest.
It knew not that
It had invaded
A suburban bulkhead that
Signified an unnatural imposition
Upon the still, mostly rural
Landscape. It was also a
Stupid, most precipitous, and
Ungainly, ugly way to gain
Access to the chilly, impersonal
Cellar that always flooded after
The balm of spring liquidated
The winter's virgin snow.

But, to me, the horrid structure
On that day housed a tiny
Treasure—a black, little gem
Neither coal nor diamond
Formed from said bitumen,
Like the smoking asphalt
Recently steamrolled to make
Way for a modern driveway
That could potentially accommodate
Three cars as big as ocean liners.

After the slaughter of trees
And extirpation of grass gave
Way to progress, it must have been
In the wake of this exciting
Activity that the mouse toppled
Down, lost its little way,
Or got stuck trying to shelter its bit
Of a body from the thunderstorm of a
Blackened and blustery

New England summer's eve.

My mother shrieked
That a rat had penetrated
The vestal hearth,
And called my father
Busy at work and on
A rotary phone. It was
So clumsy and slow,
A wonder it worked.
He answered, I know not
What. But, somehow
Apprised, I picked it up.
That little black nub,
That I thought so cute,
And sensitive too in its
Species-specific way.
I carried it into
The field, for I had
Said (many times over,
To those who refused to
Hear) that it was just a
Field mouse—not a
Rat, nor anything verminous,
And not anything venomous.
And I let the little thing go.

I nested it in the long summer
Grass deluded I could give it
A little permanent bed. Then
I felt the rain beginning to
Pelt hard, and I felt sorry for
Such a defenseless thing.
It could not have lived
Long after that, for Mother
Nature is cruel. But suburbia more
So, since domesticity demanded
It should ignorantly preside.
And that little black mouse,
That I had tried to ensure
It had survived, died
For a progress that could

Not abide anything other
Than those silly, steaming, hot-topped
Streets of a small, smothering,
Superficial, and insignificant world.

ARIADNE'S THREAD

The thread
Of Ariadne
Was meant
To find
A way
Out of
A labyrinth,
With all
Of its
Dead ends,
False beginnings,
And obviate ways.

But this Arachne needs no introduction.

On a mid-summer's eve,
When the babies went out,
I espied an amazing web, not of lies,
But of natural gossamer spent.
My kids returned, but because
So low, they did not tragically
Rent said masterpiece.

She had managed
To anchor two of her long
Threads to the porch railing,
And another to the post.
I could not see how she stayed
It up there. But she somehow knew.
Very patiently, very quietly,
She persisted around and
Around, and around and around,
Creating those perfectly elongated
Rectangles, dozens and dozens
Of them. Yet how did she know?
Mother Nature and Father Evolution
Had granted her this instinct
To build, and weave, and live,
And catch her prey.

As Zeus that night hurled his angry
Bolts, and thundered in the sky of
My country retreat, my babies
Snuggled up, and we all fell asleep.
The next morning, I noticed how the
Wind and rain had destroyed her
Elaborate gift (no trace of it
Remained). I sighed and hoped
That the little artist had survived
Somehow, somewhere, to
Weave her way again.

Minerva had nothing on her.

At the time I believed I occupied a wasted life.
But now, looking back, I see how I lived
Through quite a web of experience.

IS NEST-BUILDING AN INSTINCT?

Cf. Lowne, F.L.S., Benjamin T. "Is Nest-Building an Instinct?" Popular Science Review (1879): 274-278.

"Men are born with a special aptitude for certain acts, both mental and physical, and that mind is endowed with properties of special nature..." (278).

Someone asked me a really stupid question today.
"Is nest-building an instinct?" he squinted and scratched his
    hairy chest.
"Of course it is!" I spat. "How else could it be?"

Like the times they built a nest, between the wrapped-up hose
    and shingles,
Or in the deck chair's secure folded crook that leaned against
    the porch.
My baby Lily discerned their nestling place and sniffed them
    out with her long snout.

I creaked the folded chair slightly, just enough to peek in at
    open-beaked mouths
Looking at me to feed. When Mother Hen squawked from her
    adjacent perch,
I beat a respectful retreat.

Oh! The complications of the process,
Pine needles, and moss, and other debris.
One time I found ensconced, the fur shed by my baby, Lily.

She was my little girl, who had died that very June,
But when I looked around, those little birds showed me,
How so much smarter they really are than we.

"The importance of these facts can hardly be over-estimated, as they bear upon the theory of innate ideas, or at least of innate genius. From the foregoing experiment, the conclusion is very tempting, that the birds are endowed with special faculties and ideals..." (277-278).

MAKE WAY FOR DUCKLINGS

Cf. Konrad Lorenz and Robert McCloskey

That clever biologist at the time
Would become more famous later on.
But back then proved humble, sincere, as he
Stumbled upon a *group* of ducklings.
(He could not call them a *brood* of ducklings,
For that implied Mother Duck cared for them.)
Such here was not the case.
He insisted on being zoologically precise.

He found them abandoned and alone
By that cruel Mother Ducker.
He led them along and
Taught them to peck,
And waddle and preen,
And swam with them too.
(But they were such naturals.)

And they stuck to him like glue.
He was now Mother Duck and Father too.
Imprinting is what he called it
(Which appears here now *in print*.)

His book also did too, and after
Interviews on PBS and NPR,
And university accolades richly due,
He became very famous.
He rested comfortably on his laurels
With not much else left to do.

But what happened to the ducklings?
They would have remained a *group*,
Because he forsook them as a *brood*.
His precise language still obtained,
Even after he thought it merely
The jargon of a fool.

I swear I stumbled across them once,

Ensconced in a crystalline
Pond far from human view.

They swam as a self-contained
Enclave, motoring themselves
So sincerely and patiently by
Constantly churning little
Webbed and vascular feet.

To survive as they have done,
And to have lived as they have
Done is quite the feat.

But day after day,
And as time passes and strays,
Then they flew away.
I had not seen them leave,
And I felt sad again as I
Passed that quiet lake.

I had made way for ducklings,
Unlike that important professor,
Who had died one day, alone,
And who had grown largely unknown.

His legacy bestows his own
Findings, even though I was
The one who had made
All the difference.

That children's book be damned!
It is so far from the truth,
But that has never stopped
The opportunistic from
Exploiting the bottom line,
Especially from those
Whose hearts are pure and fine.

Just like the Common walk
And protected route
That that *brood* of ducks
Once took, and measured

Now in feet, for all the
Crowd to view.

As if they really cared or
Even knew, how hard it
Was to make way
For those precious few.

Make way! I command
You, for those are mostly
My ducklings too.

CANINE IN THE PROMISED LAND

If you take into account, how
Your sense of taste is tied
To your sense of smell, you
Would not discount your
Best friend's snout. No matter
What kind of dog food you buy,
Gourmet, wet, cold, treat, or dry,
Every dog has its day.

THE DOG DAYS OF WINTER

Incessant snowflakes fall.
Millions upon millions of them
Intent upon encumbering the way and
Making it impossible to wade through.

An obstacle, a blockage, a
Tedious circumvention
Paralyzes the region for days.
Impatience grows devoid of
The knowledge of what others have
Endured.

In the back—in the way way back—
In the yard of decay proven even
More decrepit than the city's
Shattered and glorious past,
No shadow

Of it remains. No vestige,
Just architectural jutting
Bones that signal an affront
To the prosperity of former
Days.

The wild dogs congregate as
Products of said former wealth
And privilege now abandoned, alone.
They have fallen a long way,
Through no fault of their canine own.

The memory of the local dogcatcher
Rises like a scoffing and laughing
Mist-like wraith that shames
The luxury of those decadent days.

Yet they rally, carving beds out of
The rotten wood of the former
Forest whose lungs have been
Strangled by the deluge of the

Overflowing river.

Climate change characteristically
Claiming its own, eating its young, cannibalizing
Kronos-like without a mythical precedence, or
Gloriousness, or heritage, or ambivalent, profound
Beauty.

The snow posits no obstacle for them.
Leaping, gamboling, nose to nose, they arc
And jump sniffing nose-deep this curious stuff.

They grow wanly skinny with rib-sticking
Bones, yet pant at my approach,
Recognizing a friend despite their feral fate.
One who cares also tries to help
The most helpless of a species
That should be rewarded, congratulated,
Honored, and acknowledged for
Their love and loyalty.

It's what they thrive upon,
And to take it away from
Them constitutes the most
Visceral cruelty.

A couple of enormous bags of
Dried dog food that must taste
Like dust and bought at Walmart
Given. All join the feast.

As the winds hiss and wail,
And no one is out in this hell
Of a winter gale, they retreat
To their primordial caves.

With bellies filled, they revert
To their atavistic selves.

It's all about survival.

Wolfish yet sleeping

Stuck together, snuggling,
Protecting one another after their
Owners have failed to do so.

They no longer heed only their masters' voice.

DOWN AND UP THE RABBIT HOLE

A rabbit buried in a Walmart bag
Because Sheba Inu killed another one.
Said bag would never biodegrade.
But several years later, if someone
Were to develop that land, which
Stood as a gorgeous and impossible
Garden, they'd find an intact Walmart
Bag with you in it, literally skin and bones.
A fossil in a contemporary kind of amber,
Lodged in a post-modernist landscape.

But wait! Another time and in that place
A rabbit proved most aggressive. I'd like to
Think that this one was your descendant.
Emboldened by time and natural selection,
To prove that you had never died in vain.
You ran with your quick, thick bunny thighs,
So strong and confident. You brooked no disrespect.
Your weakened and murdered ancestor lives in
This fiery bunny's blood, who attacked that crow,
A traditional and offensive consumer of carrion,
Now trying to score live rodent meat,
Swooping, descending, trying to feast on you.
Again and again, perched on the fence,
Like that poet's rook in stormy weather, or
Her unfaithful spouse's hawk in the rain.
But you defied that nasty crow, as you munched
On that simple suburban grass. Doing your quiet thing,
Even though you destroyed the neighbor's garden,
But you would have no part of it. Decency be damned.

You put up a fight, the blood in your rabbit
Veins coursing through with pride and disdain.
In your little bunny way, you conquered the
Crow, symbol of advantageous evil, and
Selfish dismay. You put up a fight, and sent
The crow flying, in more ways than one.

THE TOAD

Feeling compelled and loyal to the memory of my dead
    ancestors,
I bought flowers and mulch and a water can to ensure that the
Dead would be honored. Would pink, red, and orange
    geraniums
Be enough? They did not seem like a respectful and humble
Offering, but such was the case. A big bag of black mulch, heavy
To bear, that would nourish the dry earth of a lone cemetery.

I set to work. I dug up the small space of dense earth in front
Of the grave of my grandparents. The dirt of their plot proved
Thick and difficult to disinter, for it signified the end of the plot
Of their lives. I dug, thinking of their bones buried far beneath,
Feeling as if I were digging toward them, and that perhaps I
Committed a sin. Dishonoring the dead who should simply
Be left to rest in peace. Now I knew what RIP really meant
When before it struck me as a cartoon joke.

The sun shimmered in the low heat of a humidity-
Less day when I heard a bird above and to the right up in a tree.
I knew how Grammy and Grandpa kept birds often in a cage,
And with binoculars and an Audubon guide kept track of
The wild ones by the river's edge that they occupied.
This one whistled and sang, and as I pointed it out
To myself, it rendered itself instantly mute.

And then, what did I see? A muddy toad all
Brown in and of itself by nature borne appeared
As I dug the earth. It could not have been impacted
In the density of said ground. I took it as a sign, out of
Nowhere the precious thing appeared.

And then it hopped to the left of the gravestone,
And it looked at me in such a way. It was not afraid at all.
It rustled the dead leaves I had removed from the grave's
Plot, insistent upon registering the womb from which it sprang.

Its steady gaze did not intimidate, yet I knew that it
Meant business. Astounded and delighted, I returned

To my busy work. Geraniums and petunias all planted
In patient rows. With black mulch work done, and topped
By more thirsty water to ensure that they'd thrive, even
Though the winter's ice and snow will obliterate them
When no one is around.

The cemetery must be a cold, dark, and lonely place
In the wintertime. Perhaps a few courageous souls
Struggle to place a wreath, a poinsettia, or even
What could pass as winter flowers as a dark memorial
To their loved ones. But is it even worth it?

But in the late spring and early summer, when
Skies shine brightly blue, and the sun bakes without
Oppressive humidity, and one tans in the
Benevolent sun, a little toad, that arrived
To say hello, and function as a sign to
Indicate that those in the underworld are fine,
Disappeared behind a grave, leaving me
To wonder if it had ever been real at all.

THE DEATH OF THE MOTH

Why is the moth
Drawn toward the light
When it is no good
For it or others?

Fluttering fervidly,
Feverishly dancing,
A dervish-like in-and-out
Dance of brown-winged
Speckled dust flying and
Coming and going
To the source
Of heat.

Toward it again,
Back from it again,
To a hot and dangerous
Yellow, sallow-like glow,
Hellish and painful.

Suicidally going into the light,
Where there is peace and serenity
In the light.

The Resurrection
That begins with Death's end,
And despite the Light at
The end of the tunnel,
No God, no Jesus, just Death,
In the form of an oncoming Train.

ACORNS

Small acorned faces pressed up
Against the glass windows of a cheesy
Cracker box on its way to school,
All hope expects them to take
Root and grow. Besides, it's much
Safer than sprouting wings to fly.

JESUS FALLS THE THIRD TIME

All good things are hidden in the Cross and under the Cross. Therefore they must not be sought and cannot be understood except under the Cross. Thus I, poor little creature, do not find anything in the Scriptures but Jesus Christ and Him crucified.—Martin Luther

We were the students of Saint Praxed School.
Sister Ann Michael (who had a man's name),
Said, in spring, we're a heavenly jewel,
When the Stations of the Cross proved our aim.
At Station Nine, Jesus Falls the Third Time.
We dared not look ahead at Station Ten.
The Romans indulged themselves in great crime
As they stripped him of his fair garments then.
Jesus stands with a beautiful body,
Exposed to his groin we studied his chest.
We couldn't help but look and feel guilty.
Jesus was a man just like all the rest.
It was right and just to give Jesus praise,
Even as we lived in those lustful days.

BOXER DANCE

Tough guy, with your sleeve tattoos,
And your slicked-back Guido cut.
There's just something so beautiful
About that boxer stance you
Immediately assume any time
You feel threatened. You bob
And weave with a grace that
Transcends any violent way
You could possess, for I know
You've been hurt in the past, and
Your pugilistic instinct kicking in
Is your way to say stay away. But
It's also an involuntary defense
That belies you, who is so sweet,
Compassionate, and loving too.
Because I know that you would
Instantly dance like that for me,
Should the world threaten my way.

NARCISSUS

Writers, actors, and artists are some of the most
Narcissistic people I have ever met, that famous
Poet said. And I must agree, now that you've left me.
Oh, poof! you'll say. A matter of sour grapes, of lust
Left to decay. I never said she talked about you.

You sit in that black-and-white photograph,
Too consciously and retroactively produced, with
All of its pretentiousness, exactly like you.
Holding a dog that doesn't look real—a stuffed
Animal that approximates a semblance of a
Real self, not one you could ever do.

Good luck with that—the book shelves
Lined as if casually stored but oh so
Strategically placed. You're an
Impostor—the Red Badge of
Courage of American letters.

You'll never understand, just
What a sieve and empty vessel you are,
No matter the acclaim and the applause.
But in the silence of night, and in the
Depth of your thoughts, you know that,
Deep in the guts of your being,
You have accomplished essentially naught.

UNREQUITED

Of course that's the word you would use.
Polysyllabic, pseudo-Romanticist,
With an SAT-like finish.
Perhaps he is preoccupied.
Perhaps it isn't always about you.
But do you want to know what I know?
He apprises nothing of your existence—is
Epistemologically amputated from you.
You nobody—you ontological zero.
Such naïveté.
To think that thinking makes it so,
And that saying it makes it even more so.
You are not Jesus.
You cannot turn water into wine.
You cannot multiply fishes and loaves.
You are no miracle-worker.
I hope he has been worth it,
Because you certainly have not.

BUNNY

The first words to come to mind
Never do their due,
Which is why I must now
Express my duty to you.

One fine day,
Out in the fields,
Where we walked alone,
My kids peed and pooed.

A little puffy dot,
Breathing intensely;
Made of cotton fluff,
Speckled by gray dots,
And a few that were beigey.

You were in such distress as
My babies approached, but
They did not as usual
Tear your sweet throat.

You would have been rabbit stew.

Even Lily somehow knew
Not to throttle you.

They poked and they sniffed,
Advanced and retreated, and
Apprised of your injuries
That had you defeated.

I picked you up, a microscopic
Little puff, and placed you
In my pocket, for you
Were such small stuff.

Both Sheba and Lily,
Excited to see, and
Play with another

That suffered incessantly.

I brought you back home,
And nursed you to
Health. You were my
Project. I committed myself.

You proved much more
Dear, than anything I
Knew, except for my
Babies. You were
Part of the crew.

Now I had another buddy.
I hoped it knew I was true.
But what kind of roadkill
Could be a pet to you?
(So my selfish lover asked.
But he knew not the love
That vermin could give.)

You may have been vermin, but
I did not care. You occupied
Your niche, and replaced
One whose favor
Could no longer grace.

One whom I'd loved all
Of these years, but,
Despite all of that,
I can say here and now,
That he was really the rat.

THE RAT AND THE PEACH

On a mid-September morning,
I espied a tiny movement
In the grove of the backyard
Of the house I was renting.
I'd retreated to this hovel
(It was not in rats' alley where
The dead men lost their bones),
Because my ex had gone out
Through certain half-deserted streets
Where I could not be found.
The bit of a rat (as far as I could tell)
Gnawed at the skin of a fruit
(Peaches you might call them)
That proved sour and noxious to the taste.
(According to my neighbor's account.)
I poured the morning tea, when my
Neighbor-lady arrived, fearful of
The infestation that these
Black-Death rats could provide.
When I told her that I thought
That such pestilential filth
Could not obtain in this pastoral retreat.
She raised her cup, to her lips, took a sip
And mentioned my mistake.
"That is not what I meant at all," she said.
"That is not it at all."
She beat a hasty retreat.
And when I looked back out,
The peach seemed not affected at all
By ratty fangs, prone to eat
Dead human fingers or infant face.
(Or so they would make you think.)
I would like to believe, that on some
Level of its own, the vermin-like
Collective unconscious it may
Possess, prompted the rat to ask
Itself, "Shall I eat a peach?"

SNAKE GODDESS, MINOAN, 1600 BC

I learned about you in Dr. Staunton's art history class.
In that cavernous and dark lecture hall, where the slides
Clicked steadily away, as they did in that old day.
First, Wounded Bison, Altamira Spain, 15,000 BC, then
Herd of Horses discovered in 1879 in Lascaux, France
Singled out by the flowing line depicting their movement.
Peasant Couple Plowing, sixteenth century BC, Egypt.
Then you appeared on the scene. You certainly frightened me.
Discovered by archaeologists in Crete in 1903, with your
Genteel dress and your exposed breasts. Was that a snake on
Your head, too? But the other two uplifted in your arms
        with wrists
Grabbing each by the neck, looking as if ready to prick you.
I knew they must have been bad, diabolical emblems of Eden.
But wait! These were pre-Biblical days, that cute guy Patrick said.
(I was jealous of him.) Yes, I agreed, a much later Miltonic
        interpretation.
That's exactly right, Dr. Staunton added. The serpent is
        simply the
Cleverest, not evil. And at that later point, stood upright
        on two feet.
We all laughed at his joke. The Snake Goddess continued to
        stare us down
From the lecture hall screen, frozen in eternity, wallowing
        in fertility,
Affixing these snakes to suckle her Minoan breasts,
And then plucking them away once satiated with mother's milk.
Either way, the bosomy satisfaction the serpentines enjoyed,
Sent her slick children slithering away to conquer the earth.

MALE MUSE

He lopes along like the big, bad wolf,
And if that lupine character ever
Materialized, it would be he.
It's not as if he embodies fear,
Or a kind of rabid terror. He's a
A man of wide strides, who also
Possesses an assured solidity. He's
The one who shoulders heavy things,
And responsibilities for others. His
Threadbare blue shirt (the only one
He owns) rises at his waist when
He lifts these burdens, on the right
Side of his torso where his abdomen
Meets. He's really not all that handsome.
(This assumption rests, of course,
On the belief that physical beauty is a
Prerequisite for romantic love.) But he
Has made hearts pitter-patter, and one
(Certainly not I), approaches him
With a quivering soul and a humble
Request, "Could you get to know me?"

DUST MIXED WITH DESPAIR

*"Now is myn herte all hool, now is it oute."—Queen Midas
(from "The Wife of Bath's Tale" by Geoffrey Chaucer)*

Foolish people say
Silly things, such as,
"Karma is a bitch";
"What goes around comes around";
And "The more you want him
The less you get." But I have
Discovered quite the opposite.

In an aberration, a violation,
Of the so-called Law of Return,
I strived to hide myself from him
In a proverbial, rhetorical corner,
Where I desired he could not see me.
But, do you know what? The more I
Tried to hide, the more frequently
He appeared.

It's all about visibility.

He bespeaks poverty. The jeans
He wears always droop. Even
With a belt, I've seen his torso,
The lower series of his abs, and
The crack of his buttocks too.
He owns one threadbare blue
Shirt, part of the uniform. And
He has one pullover, and one
Hooded sweatshirt, always
Riding up to show his flesh anew.
But he acts like he doesn't know.
No shame, no humility—unconsciously
Celebrating his partial nudity.

She cares nothing for him.
Sullen, surly, sulky, she sports
Several tattoos, symbols of her

Irritability, fragility, insecurity.
She depends excessively upon him,
With no personality of her own.
He bought her chocolate-covered cherries,
Something that I would never eat, or
Ever ask him for, if he ever asked me.
But he's with her, she's with him, he's
Not with me, and, as I said, I
Am certainly not with him too.

But if he were with me,
I'd buy him new clothes,
I'd draw him a bath,
And I would work so hard
To support him too. I'd
Grocery shop in the
Dead of night if I had to.
Since he must awake before
Dawn, I'd prepare him a
Lunch and have dinner done.
I'd massage his muscles that
Would be sore and strong, his
Shoulders and chest, and
Give him other things too.

But I'm nobody—who are you?
But he is not nobody too.
When they walked away, she
Grabbed his hand, as if she
Sensed my colonization of him.
She's a stupid woman, but
Her woman's intuition pings
Upon the primordial feeling,
The last resort of the untutored.

Yet she has vanquished me,
And always will, when it
Comes to the likes of him. I sigh, I
Suffer, really no excuse
For such snobbery, since
He would not approve, and she
Succeeds. I do realize, once again,

When it comes to her, she knows her men.

I'm finished now.
She sleeps with him.
And I, a cipher, a null, a void,
A zero and the empty set, where nothing
Contains, even though it is a structure
A grammar school student can get.
(I doubt his self-indulgent girlfriend,
That parasitic lamprey eel,
Would ever have a clue.)

Emotions are personal, and
So abstract, psychological, too.
They are hardwired neurologically,
But can also weigh as heavy as lead.
Though you can't touch, or taste
Them, or see them through.
These are the moments I dread.
As I shake the dust from my sandals,
And turn to leave, I choke down
A balked desire mixed with the
Blasting heat, of desert-like despair,
That Dido knows so well, here with
Me, two queens, burning in Dante's hell.

REVELATION

To my dear, departed lover,
What profit it a man to gain the whole
World only to lose his soul? But you
Wouldn't know much about that.
With your perfect symmetry,
Tiger, tiger burning bright,
With your etched pecs
And broad-shelved shoulders
I loved to hold, too.
Oh, my dearest, how I
Loved that you stood
As my man for the time
Being. My surrogate boyfriend,
When the dark horses of
The apocalypse raged through.
In the dark of the day,
Sitting alone, I hear the
Mourning doves coo.

FISHER KING

In the Waste Land, all barren and dead,
With the Fisher King exposing his wounds
As he sat upon the shore fishing with the
Arid plain behind him, he appeared.
He irrigated, replenished, disseminated,
And spread his seed across the land.
I hadn't known this in a very long time,
But he knew how to plough the fields.
Burgeoning and unguent, his juice and
Jouissance knew just what to do. And
Now I am a product of his agricultural
Project, revivified like that sad neglected
Plant, left behind in the late summer
Greenhouse, needing just a little love so
That it could then thrive, even flourish, well
Into the winter of its personal discontent.

DEPARTURE

That time he left
Did not meet with devastation.
I had sensed it coming.
He didn't lope up to me with
His rugged confidence (as he'd
Always done before). He toddled—perhaps
More of a sway (yes, that was it)—lifted
His baseball cap, readjusted it,
(He was stalling, trying to waste time),
Rubbed the stubble on his cheek,
(He had always seemed a bit unkempt),
Looked at me, still saying nothing,
Placed his hands on my shoulders,
And finally said, "I just can't do this
Anymore."

I felt no shock.
No pain yawned inside me.
I fell into no abyss.
The temple curtain did not tear.
The dead did not rise from their graves.
The mountains never shook,
And God remained in his heaven,
Complacently dispensing mortal ways.

I said nothing.
I certainly was not going to beg him.
I didn't question softly
Why I failed? For that
Proved *my* triumph.

And I let him go.

Someone else had lured him away.

It was as if a blank, black space
Consumed me, as if stuck
In a cold, celestial vacuum.

And then I didn't care.

Just like that.
(I surprised even myself.)
For I realized, in that very moment,
How little he had valued me all along.

YOU AND YOUR WIFE

After everything, you call me
To say that nothing is good.
It didn't work out in your way.
What do you expect me to do?
You committed yourself to your wife
And your kid, about whom nothing
I knew. Master of deception and lies,
You made me love you too. For, if I
Had known, I never would have
Begun with you. Yet you approach
Me again, in your casual way, strutting
Along. You know I can't resist you. And
It's quite cruel. You know you can
Exploit me. You can act just like
Prisoners do. Manipulative, seductive,
So sexy and so manly too. It's unfair,
My dear past lover. But I am quite busy
Now. Did you think I'd collapse without
You? Tragic Trojan woes are due:
You should never speak of any mortal
As happy until he dies, and you see
Him buried in the earth, his day final.
From the gods us, misfortunes will shatter,
And such is the outcome of this matter.

CLAIM

It had been literally the third time I had started it.
Anna Karenina was finally dead, though I had
Kept her alive since at least November of 1989.
Thirty years, but who's counting?

Part 7, Chapter 31, she throws herself under a train.
So painful to me, for I had lived with her for thirty years.
I close the book as the May dusk shines,
As it always does in the approaching summer
In St. Petersburg, which freezes the year round.
Yet in summer it emits an eternal, ironic brightness.

Even her death was mean and low, as the
Countess Vronskya said. But she was worried
About her son. He was a mess because of her.
And she…she had descended into a mad irrationality
Of repulsion and disgust at her fellow man.
So non-sensical, so unneeded, so tragic.
Be it not Christian, the Countess continued,
I hate the woman for it, even in death.
She ruined everyone [her son, she means].
And she had had her revenge.

Vengeance is mine, saith the Lord.
I will repay.

And everything goes on.
Even after her death, the novel continues
For at least one hundred pages,
Even though you see her mangled corpse,
With its head unnaturally jutted back,
Still with its delicate ringlets of hair
In place, along with her real lace,
Which the maid servants recognized
As that elegant woman rushed past
Them on the platform to her death.

I cook the meal. It is simple.
Chicken breast and asparagus,

A true country feast, just like
Levin's sincere, befuddled peasants.

A hard knock on the door as I think,
Who could it be?
Followed by a subtle tap on the pane.
Stridency devolves to deference.

I open the door.
It's you.
I say nothing and
Return to my peasant feast.

You enter, shut the door,
And follow.
What are you doing? you ask.
You lean against the counter
With your arms interlocked over
Your broad and muscled
Chest, your left boot crossed
Over your right.

"I want to take you out," he says.
No.
"I want to be with you," he says.
No.
"I want you to be with me tonight."
No.

He approaches me with his
Strong, sensual saunter.
The chicken sizzles in the pan.
The asparagus steams over.

He places his hands on my hips.
In his tight jeans, he presses
His cock to mine. He sways
And looks at me so lovingly.

I take off his baseball cap.
He's a jock no longer in hiding,
And run my fingers through his hair.

"Where is your wife?" I ask.
"Don't worry about that," he says.
He stares me down.

He pulls me to him, embraces,
Kisses me, then lifts me.
He is so strong, for I am no
Twink. He lays me on the bed,
Gets on top, straddles me.
He stares at me, his eyes dancing,
Then kisses me again.
The end.

"God forgive me for everything!"
Anna Karenina screams as she
Is crushed beneath the wheels
Of that moving train, echoing
That first suicide in freezing
St. Petersburg, when she first
Met the Countess Vronskya.
(All because of *that* woman!)
As she unrelentingly soars into
The eternity of her tortured soul.

MANLY MEMORY

Every guy I saw today
Reminded me of you—
Scruffy-bearded,
Baseball-capping
Loping through
And through.

Your memory didn't
Slice my heart
Like a painful knife—
Just a reminder
I was happy
You were in my life.

THE SHUT-IN SOUL

Are there some realms which
Hitherto have been denied you?

The imaginative? That's easy enough.
The celestial? That's to be determined.

The physical...the sensual...the erotic?

Now that's a different story.

He stands before you, with his black short
Hair you'll never run your fingers through.

He looks at you with hazel eyes that
Will never gaze lovingly in yours.

He smiles at you with lips
That will never want to kiss you.

Beneath his clothes, you discern
His taut and strong muscular
Arms and chest that will never hold you.

His crotch exhibits his hot sex that
You will never experience.

Said realm sails universally off,
Brother to the arc you cannot catch,
Not of this world, and never to be yours.

The law of homogamy states like to like—
Each after its own kind.

Unlike to you, he is no longer that.
In fact, he was never that in the first place.

That's all you need to know on earth,
And all there is to know.

TWO YEARS LATER

"I shall forget you, as I said, but now,
If you entreat me with your loveliest lie
I will protest you with my favorite vow."
—Edna St. Vincent-Millay

The phone rings.
It's him.

I place *A Few Figs from Thistles*
Atop of Sadie, who is snuggled
Up beside me. She doesn't move.
It's a thin volume anyway. I take
It off and place it next to her.
She stirs contentedly, and sighs
A little whine from her throat.

She doesn't care.

I take a deep breath.

"Hello."
"Hey, babe," he says. "How are you?"
"Fine."

It has been two years, almost to the day,
And, most ironically, my birthday. The
Summer solstice, longest day of the year,
At nine o'clock, the dusk's light still peeks out
With a bright and tender abandonment.

I feel at home.

"So, what's up?" he asks.

I can hear him smoking.
"Not much," I say.

I want to ask him.
Why were you not there for me?

Why did you leave me that day for her
Whom you despised, when you knew
What I was going through?

And I was alone.

I want to rage and fulminate.

But I don't.
I have learned the hard lessons
Of years past, and no longer
Wish to appear weak
In front of my enemies.

For they will always use
It against me.

And now, when she's gone,
A paragon of dingy working-class
Reluctance, who only stayed around
As long as he could support her.
And now that he can't, he calls.

Such transparent ignorance,
Offensiveness. How does he
Even think he can deceive me?

He is no puzzle. No set of
Interlocking pieces needing to
Be put together to form a whole,
To render the fragments a
Discernible clarity and vision.

He has never been that
Sophisticated, and he never
Will be, despite his pretensions
To greatness, he has repeatedly
Failed over and over.

"Can I come over?" he asks.

I hear him take a deep drag, of
Cigarette or pot or aught.
I look down at Sadie, snuggled
In the dusk of a light summer's
Night.

Edna St. Vincent-Millay sits
By my side. I know she would
Acquiesce with her truest vow
To the falsest of his lies.

I emit the longest of sighs.

"Sure," I say. "Come on over."
"Great!" he says. "See you soon."

I know when he arrives what will happen.
I know it will be wrong when I stay true.
But please don't judge me until
The same has happened to you.

IMAGE

Dead leaves, scuttling across the pavement
In the early dark of that first Friday after
The clocks fall back. Yellowed, browned,
And full of death, you metamorphose their
Dance as the cold bites your cheeks and
Infects your bones. But you think of yourself
As too young for that. But his memory arises,
Even though it has been a few years, for the
Autumn bleakness shrouded his last days.
Sense memories, unavoidable, dredge up
Those thoughts. You can't help it. And
Although it feels like years, your existence
Reinforces the mortality of an immortality,
(Or should one say immorality), that we all,
Unfortunately, (or perhaps fortunately),
Labor under as we shoulder our lives.

MY GOOD DAY DONE

My hopes have been dashed, many times in life,
It's a wonder I even persever.
I muck my way through the sludge and the strife,
Thinking I somehow should have known better.
I issue a grievance, a gripe, a grief,
To smash an ideological block.
I rage at the gods—it's a tired old beef,
But low murmurs come—stuff it with a sock.
Some day when old, and gray, and full of sleep,
I'll recall this now, as Virgil once said,
And smile at the promise I thought to keep:
To satisfy Mammon before I'm dead.
And then I shall rest, my good day done,
And cherish this win, which is really none.

A GRAVE

Before I died,
I said to him,
Who was not
Ever there for me,
"As long as I am not
Tortured, mutilated,
Raped, or bludgeoned
To death, I will feel
That I have died
With a little dignity."

He chose to bury me,
In his strange way,
In an unmarked grave.
As if I were a perpetrator
Of unspeakable crime,
Aware of his untoward ways,
Who should best be silenced,
And put away, along with the fish,
Near the briny and cold-hearted bay.

GERTRUDE STEIN NARRATES A NURSERY RHYME

In her own way.

1. **Jack and Jill went up the hill.**

Jack and Jill went up a hill.
Jack and Jill went up this hill, not that hill.
Jack and Jill go up a hill.
Jack and Jill are going up the hill, but would have been going up that hill, had they not been
    going up this hill.
A hill.
Jack and hill go up a Jill.

2. **To fetch a pail of water.**

To fetch, fetch, fetches, fetching, fetching a fetching pail.
Fetching a pail, fetching a pale pail.
A pale Jack and a pale Jill fetch a pail.
Fetching a pale pail of pale water.
A pale Jack and a pale Jill fetch a pale pail of pale water.

3. **Jack fell down and broke his crown.**

Jack fell.
He did fall down and broke a crown.
It was not a king's crown, or even a crown of a queen.
No, it was not that.
It was a crown.
His head? No, a tooth?
No.
It was a crown.
That Jack fell down and broke.
Jack fell and broke his crown.
Now let me tell you about his broken crown.
It was damaged.

4.   And Jill came tumbling after.

Jill tumbles.
Jill tumbles after.
Jill tumbles and is tumbling after.
She tumbles as she tumbles after.
It is her thing.
To tumble.
Jill tumbles after and it is a very good thing.
Jill's tumbling after is a very good thing.
Because Jill tumbles after.
Jill tumbles, has tumbled, is always tumbling.
Tumbling is Jill's thing.
She continues to tumble, now and before and after.
Jill tumbles before, during, and after.
Jill tumbles.

TO NEVER KNOW ME

How do I justify the pain
I feel when all the boys
Run away from me in their prime?
Shirtless and sweaty, they
Revel in their physicality.
At night, their good games begun,
They meet the women of the street.
And I in my parlor, imprisoned by crinoline,
Long to see their sinewy bodies.
But I have pledged to one,
Who knows not a woman's needs.
The empty marriage bed lies,
And I am unable to see,
Living with a limp fish
Who loves unsatisfyingly.
The dirty boys run by,
And they hold a hard stake in me.
So, I shall take a swim
To bathe myself in briny sea,
Wishing that those raucous boys somehow
Knew I would rather drown, than be
Betrothed to one, who shall never know me.

FELINE-ICIDE

Emily Dickinson, America's poetic sweetheart,
Really hated cats. Her sister Vinnie, whom
She loved so, kept them around for her own
Satisfaction. Emily loved Lavinia but took a
Kind of perverse pleasure in her sister's
Simple incomprehension of her genius.
So, one cat she pickled in the cellar,
Another she allowed to be de-tailed,
(Quite literally and weirdly—it really
Makes me mad she could be so cruel!)
You would think that Emily would
Never act that way, yet it is simply
Another example of an assumed
Christian morality, which she
Characteristically fought in her poetry.

Such poetic genius—
Who Felt a Funeral—in her Brain—
And heard a Fly Buzz—when she died—
And died for Beauty until—the Moss
Covered up her Lips—Because she could
Not Stop for Death—

Also killed the family's pets.

I guess she could be catty like that—Sometimes.

THE NATURES OF THE BEASTS

"There was a youth whose name was Thomas Granger; he was servant to an honest man of Duxbury, being about 16 or 17 years of age. ...He was this year detected of buggery (and indicted for the same) with a mare, a cow, two goats, five sheep, two calves, and a turkey. ...He was cast by the jury, and condemned, and after executed about the 8th of September 1642. A very sad spectacle it was; for first the mare, and then the cow, and the rest of the lesser cattle, were killed before his face, according to the law, Leviticus 20:15, and then he himself was executed."
—*History of Plymouth Plantation* by William Bradford

Now, I do not know, but can imagine, that Thomas Granger
Was a stud and sexy too, who needed to ventilate
The frustrations of his young libido. What did it matter?
Nowadays, and after the stolid Freud, we know that
Young guys have their ways. To get off with five sheep,
Two goats, a calf or two, horrified the Separatists,
But why did they separate too? Still, the Pilgrims
Condemned the sex of this boy, who was most likely
Alone, abandoned, with no parents to boot. What
Role model had he? Untutored, horny, and making his way,
He just came along to enjoy his sexual day. First the turkey,
Prepared for the Thanksgiving feast, with a delicious sauce
And other proteins to eat. Then he witnessed before him
The animals slewed, then thrown in a pit the stud also laid.
Oh, now it makes no sense to condemn a boy for his sex.
Yes, it's strange, but Thomas Granger needed love too.
Whether a cow, a goose, or his favorite ewe, he has
Made great history, now read by scholars like you.

THE SCARLET LETTER

Having cast off kings and queens,
The Puritans knew just what to do.
Finding themselves in the strange New World,
They paid stern Yaweh his due.
Hester Prynne lived among them
Abandoned and alone by the old
Deformed Chillingworth who could
Not perform, and struck his
Young wife as zero at the bone.
It took him forever to make the trek
To the Bay Colony, for such an expert
With his knowledge of herbs, trees, and shrubs
Does not impress his fertile young wife.
So it was no wonder that with Dimmesdale she lay,
And conceived his child with whom he'd never play.
Shamed on the scaffold one burning summer's day,
The mother held Baby Pearl, the jewel of her sin,
And encountered the contempt of those no better than she.
The Scarlet Letter that Hester wore like a proud badge of shame
Had endowed her with a secret knowledge of
The guilt and sin of her fellow men.
Many maidens before her had buried babes born too soon,
As well as sodomites who practiced each noon
When all were at meeting or out in the field.
She had defied the great wrath of God,
So did they say, but she was most innocent, come what may.
But history has a way of righting such wrongs,
And Hester became a Sibyl of throngs.
Through the years, jaded women, disappointed maidens
And such ilk, sought her wise counsel, like an old mother's milk.
She lived by the sea in that same cottage of yore,
Whither she'd been banished years ago as a whore.
Pearl went abroad and married nobility,
And took care of her mom, embroidering contentedly
In her brine-bespattered cottage next to the sea.

THE BROOKSBY VILLAGERS
ca. 1626 to the present

In Brooksby Village,
Now Peabody,
The Indians attacked,
The whites from the sea.

The magistrates ordered,
And commanded around,
These heathens be killed,
But carnage redounds.

They fasted and prayed,
And by God's goodwill,
Shared blankets infected,
And smallpox did kill.

Some decades later,
Near century's end,
The children all gathered,
As Tituba's friend.

With egg whites they scryed,
Whose goodwives they'd be,
And listened to voices,
Of dead family.

Mistresses of Satan,
Now tortured their dreams.
They shrieked as possessed,
Those evil hags' names.

Legend has had it,
That their hanging tree,
Stood right on this spot,
Here in Peabody.

Now covered in flowers,
And landscaped galore,
The path leads straight up,

To the Brooksby Village door.

Its denizens' wealth,
Now clearly affords,
The leisure to silence,
Memory's mystic chords.

They're assisted in living,
The staff does its part,
And right down the road,
The shuttle stops at Walmart.

They creep up to cashiers,
With snacks and Depends,
And reboard the bus,
Their day at an end.

With Indians dead,
The witches all gone,
In the great dining room,
The villagers throng.

Most not with this knowledge,
Of said turbulent past,
They sit down to savor,
Their quiet repast.

If history repeats,
Such here's not the case.
But struggles are conquered,
The ones we all face.

The hearse comes and goes,
An ambulance, too.
To find peace in rest,
The last thing to do.

VIRGIN QUEEN

"The papal emissaries have arrived,
On behalf of the Prince of Aragon."
"Show them in," the Queen of Avicenne sighed.
Not married yet? You need to have a son.
It's your maiden, royal duty to do,
To secure the Holy Roman Empire.
Marriage will save, your tiny kingdom too.
But she was not barren, he could not sire
The children her loyal subjects had been.
Famine had struck, but now her fields were ploughed.
Release pigs and cows! Let fly the last hen!
Open the granaries! Wheat made to flour!
She reigned alone, as Queen Marie to take
Every good measure, to let them eat cake.

THE MONKS OF THE ORDER OF SAINT JEROME

It was the best kept secret
That sodomy routinely occurred
In that monastery. Austere Jerome,
Their patron saint, who demanded
Celibacy, was mocked by its denizens,
Cavorting nocturnally in sexual spree.
By day the prayers and chants were their due,
Intermixed with simple meals of gruel.

At night when lights singed out,
Their flagellant whips became sadistic tools.
Self-punishment meant to tame the flesh,
Converted to sexual satiety at another's behest.
Depravity signaled the goal of the game
With altar boys subjected to pederast shame.
Divine intervention, the stuff of old myth,
Hurled lightning bolts on a hot summer's day.
The dry timbers ignited and burnt to the ground
The monastery mired in surprising sin.

It is said that the decadence and debauchery
Of the Roman Empire signaled its decline.
The western world of the medieval era,
Direct descendant of a sinful Rome,
And despite its holy presumptuousness
Naturally proved to be no different.

NOAH AND THE ARK

As humble Noah once proclaimed,
Or perhaps even prophesied
Given that Old Testament way,
To that stiff-necked and
Back-sliding people as the
Raindrops began to pelt
For forty days and forty nights:
"Once the door is closed," the
Old man wheezed and pleaded,
"I cannot open it again."

And the old man would
Live for several hundred
More years. With Uxor and
His sons, one of which
Committed a grave misdeed
Against him when drunk
With wine (which wasn't so bad).
He had just saved the entire world.
After all, how many humans can
Claim that they possess the drive,
Determination, as well as the
Stick-to-it-iveness to accomplish
Something like that? I mean,
Building an ark? Who can top that?

But the animals brooked not
This human ignorance and
Filial insubordination.
In their own genetic
Diversity, they knew
They would never be accused
Of such an abomination.

All of them of the said earth then.
Triceratops, polar bear, and hen,
Amebae, hippopotamus, and cockatiel,
Those black-plague-infested rats, and
Fashionably prevalent flesh-eating bacteria too.

Of course, all of them didn't
Inhabit the area around Mount
Ararat back then. But that's not
The point. Most know that's true.

What's important, and for you
To know, is that these dumb
Animals instinctively listened,
While so-called rational humans
Refused to heed the ways of a man
Who knew how not to go astray.

ULYSSES

Ulysses, or Odysseus, whatever your name is,
You're an overrated loser. Know that Hecuba,
Queen of Sorrows, hates you for her concubinage.
But that's your *modus operandi*, isn't it, after all?
From the Kyklopes and Calypso and Circe, where
Your men were rightly turned into swine, to the
Siren Song—do you think they cared that you
Withstood them? Bane of sophomoric world
Literature students, forced to study your banality,
You are no hero. Compared to Hector and the
Trojans too, you are a narcissist, hedonist, and
Brainless fool. As patient Penelope waits, and
Weaves her way without you, she's probably
Much happier. Unraveling her tapestry day
In and day out, it's not to fend off those lusty
Bachelors, but to prolong the absence of
Your amorousness. No one waited for your
Return. No one cared what you would do.
So, home to Ithaca and Telemachus, lounge
In your chair and remember the satiety
Of lotus-eating fiends, with whom you should
Have stayed, since you are nothing but a zero too.

EURIPIDES' MEDEA
431 BCE

Barbarian princess, who left her home
And killed her own kin, so that Jason could
Steal the Golden Fleece, and on the sea foam
Scatter fraternal body parts. She would
Go to this extent, the witch that she was,
To appease her man, who left her for one
Virgin princess, for Creon's daughter does
Not yet know the marriage bed. But one sun
Is all the witch asked to stave off exile.
She makes amends and sends the golden dress,
Her soon-to-be-slain sons offer it while
It burns and poisons Creon and princess.
Jason wailed, and cursed the cruel Medea.
Helios sent *deus ex machina*.

THE END

A life of rich mentality,
Transcending all reality,
Just like Wallace Stevens
Wrote.
An imagination,
Needed
Something to do.
Now I move on,
With no
Further
Thought,
Of you.

REINCARNATED

My Master enslaved me.
I now reign Queen Supreme.
In this life, I find
Myself in-between.
Neither prosperous nor poor,
Neither wicked nor saint,
I'm cosmically content,
To pay a low rent.
Life is expensive,
And I am not rich.
But if I've learned aught,
And through spans of time,
It is as such: that I've fought
To be honest, to live
Simple and true.
To be who I am, which is just
Myself, and with enough grace,
A queen without a crown.

ABOUT ATMOSPHERE PRESS

Atmosphere Press is an independent, full-service publisher for excellent books in all genres and for all audiences. Learn more about what we do at atmospherepress.com.

We encourage you to check out some of Atmosphere's latest releases, which are available at Amazon.com, Barnes & Noble, and via order from your local bookstore:

Big Man Small Europe, poetry by Tristan Niskanen

In the Cloakroom of Proper Musings, a lyric narrative by Kristina Moriconi

Lucid_Malware.zip, poetry by Dylan Sonderman

The Unordering of Days, poetry by Jessica Palmer

It's Not About You, poetry by Daniel Casey

A Dream of Wide Water, poetry by Sharon Whitehill

Radical Dances of the Ferocious Kind, poetry by Tina Tru

The Woods Hold Us, poetry by Makani Speier-Brito

My Cemetery Friends: A Garden of Encounters at Mount Saint Mary in Queens, New York, nonfiction and poetry by Vincent J. Tomeo

Report from the Sea of Moisture, poetry by Stuart Jay Silverman

The Enemy of Everything, poetry by Michael Jones

The Stargazers, poetry by James McKee

The Pretend Life, poetry by Michelle Brooks

Minnesota and Other Poems, poetry by Daniel N. Nelson

Interviews from the Last Days, sci-fi poetry by Christina Loraine

the oneness of Reality, poetry by Brock Mehler

ABOUT THE AUTHOR

Philip J. Kowalski has taught courses in critical thinking and American literature at Wake Forest University and the University of North Carolina, Greensboro. He lives on the North Shore of Massachusetts.